HAWAii

HAWAii

PHOTOGRAPHY BY MIKE SEDAM
TEXT BY SUZAN C. HALL
FOREWORD BY PATTIE COON LANDRETH

GRAPHIC ARTS CENTER PUBLISHING COMPANY   PORTLAND, OREGON

International Standard Book Number 1-55868-063-2
Library of Congress Number 91-71224
© MCMXCI by Graphic Arts Center Publishing Company
P.O. Box 10306 • Portland, OR 97210
All rights reserved. No part of this book
can be reproduced by any means
without written permission of the publisher.
President • Charles M. Hopkins
Editor-in-Chief • Douglas A. Pfeiffer
Managing Editor • Jean Andrews
Designer • Robert Reynolds
Cartographer • Manoa Mapworks, Inc.
Typographer • Harrison Typesetting, Inc.
Printer • Dai Nippon Printing Company
Printed and bound in Hong Kong

TABLE OF CONTENTS

Frontispiece: Locally known as Tunnels, this beach is called beautiful by all who visit. Tunnels is located just east of the Nāpali Coast near Hāʻena on the island of Kauaʻi.

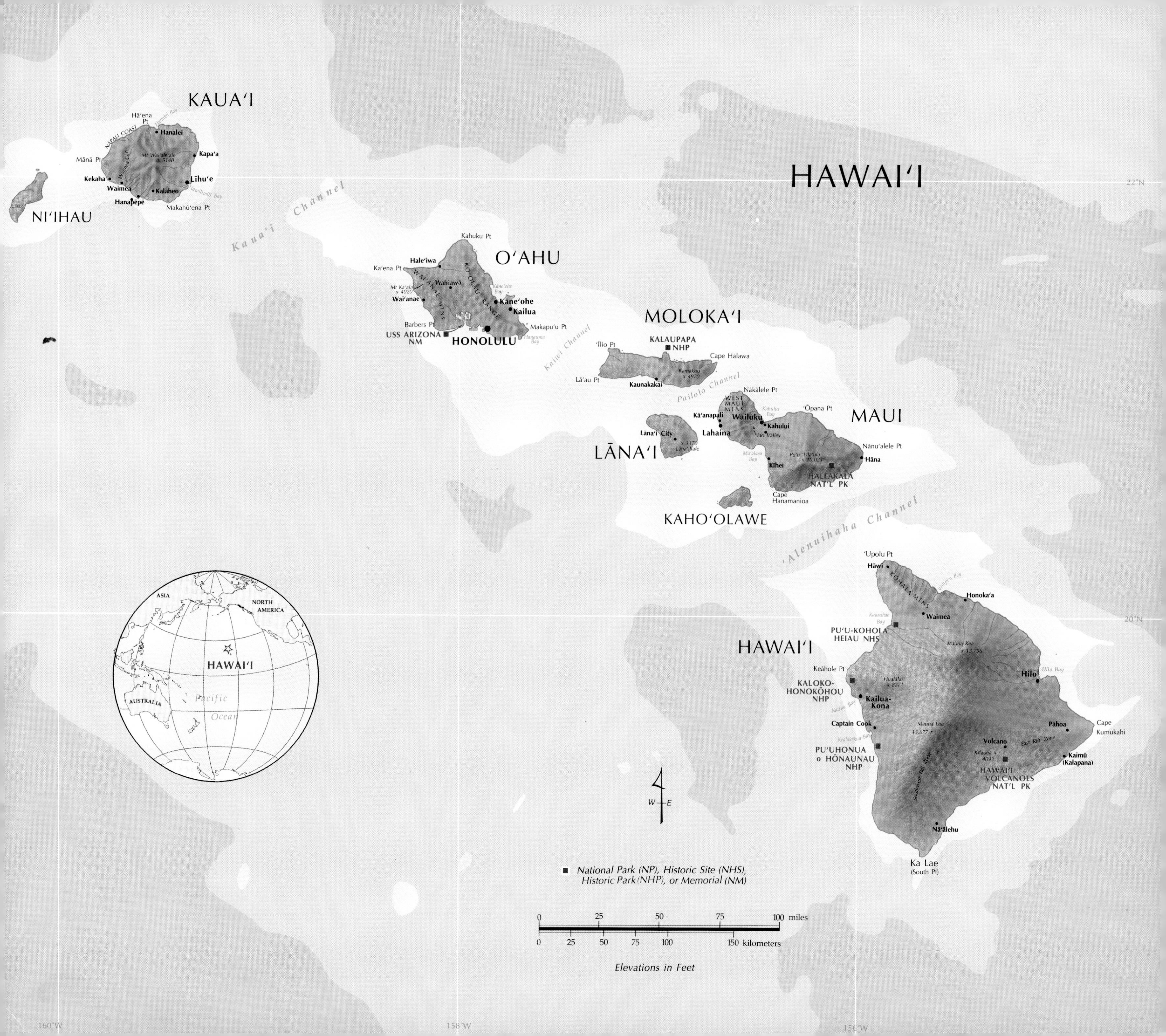

HAWAI'I

KAUA'I

Hā'ena Pt
Hanalei
Kapa'a
Līhu'e
Mt Wai'ale'ale 5148
Kekaha
Waimea
Kalāheo
Hanapēpē
Makahū'ena Pt
Mānā Pt
NĀPALI COAST
Waimea Canyon

NI'IHAU

Kaua'i Channel

O'AHU

Kahuku Pt
Ka'ena Pt
Hale'iwa
Wahiawā
WAI'ANAE MTS
Mt Ka'ala 4020
Wai'anae
Barbers Pt
USS ARIZONA NM
HONOLULU
KO'OLAU RANGE
Kāne'ohe
Kailua
Makapu'u Pt
Kāneohe Bay
Kailua Bay
Waimānalo Bay

MOLOKA'I

'Ilio Pt
Cape Hālawa
KALAUPAPA NHP
Kamakou
Kaunakakai
Lā'au Pt

Pailolo Channel
Kalohi Channel

LĀNA'I

Lāna'i City
Lāna'ihale 3370

MAUI

Nānu'alele Pt
Hāna
'Opana Pt
Nākālele Pt
WEST MAUI MTS
Pu'u Kukui 5788
Wailuku
Kahului
Kā'anapali
Lahaina
Kīhei
HALEAKALĀ NAT'L PK
Pu'u 'Ula'ula 10,023
'Īao Valley
Kahului Bay
Mā'alaea Bay
Cape Hanamanioa

KAHO'OLAWE

'Alenuihāhā Channel

HAWAI'I

'Upolu Pt
Hāwī
KOHALA MTS
Honoka'a
Waimea
Mauna Kea 13,796
Hilo
Hilo Bay
PU'U-KOHOLA HEIAU NHS
Kawaihae Bay
Keāhole Pt
KALOKO-HONOKŌHAU NHP
Kailua-Kona
Kailua Bay
Captain Cook
Kealakekua Bay
PU'UHONUA o HŌNAUNAU NHP
Hualālai 8271
Mauna Loa 13,677
Kona Coast
Volcano
Kīlauea 4093
HAWAI'I VOLCANOES NAT'L PK
Pāhoa
Kaimū (Kalapana)
Cape Kumukahi
East Rift Zone
Southwest Rift Zone
Nā'ālehu
Ka Lae (South Pt)
Waipi'o Bay

● National Park (NP), Historic Site (NHS),
■ Historic Park (NHP), or Memorial (NM)

Elevations in Feet

0   25   50   75   100 miles
0   25   50   75   100   150 kilometers

N
W—E
S

NORTH AMERICA
ASIA
HAWAI'I
Pacific Ocean
AUSTRALIA

Fishing near the spot where Captain Cook landed on the south shore near Waimea in 1778

FOREWORD

When my family first came to Hawaii, it was intended as a temporary stopover before sailing down to Easter Island, New Zealand, and Australia. We had just completed two years of sailing from Alaska down to Mexico, Central America, Ecuador, The Galapagos Islands, and the Marqueses Islands. This trip was the fulfillment of a dream my dad had had for many years.

After spending thirty years in the charter business in Alaska, my dad and two brothers, with the help of many friends, built *Trilogy*, a fifty-foot trimeran sailboat, and we took off for the adventure of a lifetime.

When we first arrived in the Islands, we decided to spend a few months exploring, just as we had done in many other places we had visited. It was fun to visit an island and see how very different each is from the others.

We first landed in Hilo on the Big Island of Hawaii. After coming from the subtropics, it was a truly magnificent sight to see palm trees along the beach, with snow-covered Mauna Kea in the background.

We spent several months on each island, sailing into hidden bays to spend time snorkeling, hiking, and enjoying the non-commercial parts still available to the adventuresome. We finally determined we liked Maui best and decided to spend more time there. That was twenty years ago! We never finished the rest of our cruise to points farther south. Instead, we began taking visitors from the island of Maui to discover the island of Lāna'i. As my dad said many times, "I always said that if I ever found paradise, I was going to stay there and never leave, and I've found mine."

Even though I have visited some of the most beautiful and lush places in the world, I still believe Hawaii incorporates the best of the tropical South Pacific along with the best of being part of the United States. You feel as though you have visited another country without having actually done so. You don't have to change money or language, and you can even drink the water.

I fell in love with Hawaii very quickly, but I also found that the pull the Islands have on me has only increased over the years. It is truly a magical place! Everything about it makes my senses come alive. From the brilliant blue of the ocean to the intoxicating scent of flowers, from the cascading waterfalls to the music, culture, and people, no other state has such mystery and charm.

I'm in love with the Islands. If you hold Hawaii in your heart—whether because you love to visit or dream of going someday—you will appreciate how Mike Sedam has captured her essence.

Mike has the ability to convey through the camera lens his own love of Hawaii. Working on assignment for major airlines, resorts, and cruise lines, Mike has photographed the most beautiful places in more than seventy-four countries and every state in the United States—and still, he says he would choose to vacation in Hawaii.

Much of Hawaii's grandeur remains unviewed because of its inaccessibility. The Islands are volcanic, and roads may go only around the perimeter of an island, leaving many beautiful parts of each island virtually unseen by most people.

To bring you the best of his landscape and aerial photography, Mike has hiked, driven, and flown by helicopter into the remote valleys, getting as close as possible to three-thousand-foot waterfalls and capturing the beauty of tropical flowers and ferns that tenaciously cling to the walls of near-vertical cliffs.

I have hiked quite a few of the valleys in Hawaii, and it is worth every bit of effort to reach the top of a ridge and view the lush vista that unfolds below.

I had lived on Maui a number of years before I decided to take a helicopter flight to view the hidden beauties from that perspective. I could not believe how much of Hawaii I had never really seen.

I wish everyone who visits Hawaii could have the incredible adventure of flying into the depths of each island to see once-inhabited valleys where now only the ancient *heiau*—lava rocks placed in a rectangular shape and once used for worship—remind us of the civilizations of long ago.

The beauty of Hawaii can surely be enjoyed by lying on the beach and cooling off in the ocean; this peacefulness is the very reason many, if not most, come to Hawaii. But there is so much more to Hawaii. Along with her peacefulness and natural gentleness, there is a violent and unforgiving part, not only historically, but also in her fiery beginnings and continuing periodic outbursts.

As beautiful and picturesque as are many of the resorts in the Islands, nothing compares with the majesty and artistry of nature. When visitors come to Hawaii and spend all their time within the controlled atmosphere of a resort, never venturing out to see and experience the true Hawaii, they have surely missed her heart.

Mike shares with you, through the pages of this book, the many faces of Hawaii, from her rugged, time-hewn beauty to her still-remaining, fragile, delicate balance. You will see her changing moods, from rainstorms to rainbows, from brilliant sunlight and sparkling ocean to spewing volcanoes and torrential waterfalls. And you will find revealed the hidden face from the ancient past, which she shows to only a privileged few, along with the face of the present, bursting forth with life as she continues to create new parts of herself.

PATTIE COON LANDRETH

Kalalau Valley, Kōkeʻe State Park from Kalalau Lookout

INTRODUCTION

. . . Near each other a group of islands spreads out like a flock of birds.
Leaping up are the divided places. Lifted far up are the heavens.
Polished by striking, lamps rest in the sky.
Presently the clouds move, the great sun rises in splendor,
mankind arises to pleasure, the moving sky is above.

CREATION, FROM AN ANCIENT HAWAIIAN CHANT

The Hawaiians had lived on these Islands for more than a millennium before the first European set foot on their shores. How the first settlers found these tiny dots of land is a matter of speculation—this rough jade necklace, tossed in mid-Pacific, is farther from other land than anywhere else on earth.

Those first Polynesian adventurers probably sailed up from the Marqueses, navigating without instruments over two thousand miles of open sea. When their great, double-hulled canoes reached Hawaii, about A.D. 500, they found a gentle climate, an abundance of plant life, and shores teeming with fish. But in this almost-paradise there were no animals, save the monk seal and the bat, and no plants that provided staple food.

Apparently those first adventurers had the foresight to bring their staples—dogs, pigs, and chickens, and important plants like taro, cane, breadfruit, and paper mulberry for making *kapa* cloth.

Generations came and went, and the people continued to till the soil and fish the sea, using tools of stone, bone, and wood. They had no written language, but they developed a rich and complex culture. They shared their goods, and even their children. They were in touch with the land, regarding it as a living thing.

Then, in 1778, Captain James Cook arrived, and everything began to change. Among the *ali'i*, Native nobles who welcomed Cook, was a forceful young chief called Kamehameha, "The Lonely One." A *kahuna*, a prophet, had foreseen his future at birth, calling him a "killer of chiefs." A political strategist as keen as any in history, Kamehameha spent the next three decades bringing all the Islands under his rule, then guided his kingdom diplomatically through the mine fields on the way to Western Civilization.

Once discovered, the Islands attracted all manner of attention. Poets wrote odes to the "noble savage," failing to understand that Hawaiians were really neither. Shipfuls of sailors and whalers made the Islands a regular port of call. Missionaries flocked in to educate the Natives, give them a new god, and convince them to cover their bronzed bodies with incongruous western attire.

No economic opportunity was overlooked. Sugar barons, cattle ranchers, and pineapple planters sized up the land, dreamed big dreams of economic success, and imported laborers from all over the world to make them come true. The once-tranquil, homogeneous Islands became a cultural melting pot.

American interests in the Islands grew, the old culture faded in the face of modern ways, and the monarchy's influence declined. Hawaii moved inexorably toward annexation and finally incorporation, in 1959, as the nation's fiftieth state.

How have these small, easy-going Islands integrated so much change? In the spirit of "Aloha"—that all-encompassing greeting/good-by/love word that literally translates *Alo*, "to face" and *ha*, "the breath of life"—they have taken it all in and made it their own.

None of those things we call "Hawaiian" were to be found in ancient Hawaii—no flowers, no music, no hula girls, no pineapple, no sarongs. Leis were made of leaves and berries, chants were monotones accompanied by drums, and only men could dance the sacred hula. Pineapples were unknown, and clothing was ti leaves and *kapa* cloth. But Hawaiians were quick to absorb new ideas and give them their own stamp. What would our image of tropical paradise be without flower leis, swaying hips, and the music of a slack-key guitar?

Paradise is, as it has always been, where you choose to find it. The unspoiled land was beautiful when those first adventurers arrived by canoe, but to survive they had to make some additions. So Hawaii has added, accepted, and adapted; and in the process, it has become a veritable cultural kaleidoscope. That only makes paradise more interesting.

The overwhelming natural beauty of the islands has not changed, nor has their capacity to seduce the senses. The air is soft and fragrant; the sea, warm and azure blue; the sand, golden and soft. The vistas are vast and glorious; the sunsets, vibrant beyond belief.

Mark Twain was right. This is, simply, "The loveliest fleet of islands anchored in any sea."

Nāpali Coast

Ancient Hawaiians believed that the peak of Mount Waiʻaleʻale, the cloud-shrouded, 5,150-foot volcano which forms the heart of the island of Kauaʻi, was the meeting place of the gods.

Mists which always hang over Waiʻaleʻale, the mountain of "rippling waters," mark the wettest spot in the world. The trade winds from the Pacific, funnelled by the Anahola Mountain Range to the north and the Hāʻupu Range to the east, dump nearly 500 inches of rain per year into its crater, creating an other-worldly place called Alakaʻi Swamp. From Alakaʻi, seven rivers fan out, rippling and falling, to carry the rainwater back to the sea.

In Alakaʻi are plants and birds that exist nowhere else on earth. One of its trees is the only remaining nesting place of the ʻoʻo ʻaʻa, a slender, slate-gray bird that once thrived on all the Islands. Its flamboyant yellow leg feathers were woven into the cloaks and helmets worn by Hawaiian royalty. The birds were caught with nets and sticky wands, then released after they had been relieved of their colored feathers. It took as many as four hundred fifty thousand feathers, plucked from eighty thousand birds and painstakingly woven into a net backing, to make a single velvety cloak. Some think that the style and red-and-yellow color scheme of Hawaiian royalty's capes and helmets suggest that Spaniards made a stop in the Islands long before Captain Cook.

Through the century and a half before contact between the Islands and the outside world, the government on all the Islands remained in the hands of the local chiefs. Order was maintained by a rigid *kapu* "taboo" system.

Society was stratified. The lines between the *aliʻi*, the ruling class; the *makaʻāinana*, the working class; and the *kauwā*, the untouchables, were clearly defined. Over time, the advantages of privilege became visible. Better food, easier living, and inter-marriage among the *aliʻi* created a class of powerful, handsome people who were often more than six feet tall.

Settled early and set slightly apart from the other islands, Kauaʻi had a proud reputation. Its chiefs were considered descendents of the gods, and were the most revered of all *aliʻi*.

When Kamehameha the Great tried to conquer Kauaʻi, storms and plagues defeated his invasion attempts. Finally, in 1810, he coaxed the island and its neighbor, Niʻihau, into his kingdom by diplomacy. His lever was the promise not to disrupt the island's lucrative sandalwood trade.

Hawaii's early history can only be guessed from archeological clues, since no written records exist. Hawaiians had a rich store of oral history and chants, passed on as *mele* from generation to generation. But in this oral heritage, fact and myth were a heady mix. To explain the mysteries of the earth with which they lived so closely, Hawaiians often blurred the distinctions between animate and inanimate, myth and reality, man and the gods.

The rich, melodious langauge of Hawaii was not transcribed to paper until after the missionaries arrived in 1820. Eager to give their new charges the Bible to read, these earnest churchy scholars set about capturing the spoken word phonetically, voting democratically among themselves when they disagreed about what letters to use. In the end, they arrived at an alphabet of only twelve letters, the consonants H, K, L, M, N, P, and W, plus the five vowels, which were given their Latin sounds. The organic sounds and expressive rhythms of the Hawaiian tongue, transcribed with this limited alphabet, became lengthy, vowel-filled words which are a considerable challenge to pronounce or tell apart.

Competing with the missionaries for the Native souls was a grand pantheon of gods and goddesses that would have put the Greeks to shame. The four supreme gods were *Kāne*, the great procreator; *Kū*, who held power over rain, growth, battle, and sorcery; *Kanaloa*, the healer, who held sway over the ocean and its winds; and *Lono*, the benevolent god of harvests, with power over the thunder, clouds, and wind.

Magical beings of lesser stature numbered at least four hundred thousand more. Magic could touch anyone or anything. Its power, or *mana*, could be anywhere. All nature was alive. Rocks could grow and procreate. Supernatural beings could take any form.

The island of Kauaʻi, it is said, is where the Menehunes still make their home. Little people like the Leprechauns, they work in secret and can complete prodigious tasks overnight, asking only one shrimp each day in pay. They are given credit for the fine stonework in the Menehune Ditch, an aqueduct in the Waimea Valley. Only ruins of this great aqueduct remain now.

Legend says the Menehunes also built the Alakoko Fishpond, upriver from harbor at Nāwiliwili, using stones passed hand-to-hand from Makaweli, some twenty-five miles away. Who were the ancient stonemasons, really? History and myth are so mingled that the truth may never be known. They may have been descendants of the island's earliest settlers, Marquesans subjugated by the larger, more powerful Tahitians who arrived centuries later. Or they may simply have been the lowest class among the ancient Hawaiians, physically smaller, who were therefore relegated to virtual serf-status.

A favorite among the lesser magical beings was Pele, the fire goddess, who was fond of appearing in human form. The people of Kauaʻi believed she spent some time on their north shores. One story says that Pele stopped at Hāʻena when she first set out, as a young goddess, to look for a home. But her digging stick struck water, creating the coastal Wet Caves. She moved on, finally settling on the island of Hawaii, where she could keep a fire pit burning. She is also said to have appeared once as a beautiful young girl and visited the hula festival on Hāʻena's Kēʻē Beach. She fell in love with a handsome young Kauaʻi Chief, Lohiau, and caused a great deal of difficulty.

West of Hāʻena is the spectacular coastline known as Nāpali, "The Cliffs." Rugged walls of lava rise a sheer three thousand feet, making its valleys and rough shores almost inaccessible. Its remote valleys were once populated by hundreds, perhaps thousands, of Hawaiians, who peacefully tilled their taro fields and fished the sea. They hiked the daunting terrain with ease, and symbiotic relationships developed between settlements like Nuʻalolo-ʻāina (ʻāina means land) and Nuʻalolo-kai (kai means sea). The valleys are now deserted, and the logs and ladders which once joined the hanging valleys with the sea have long since rotted through.

Just to the east of Hāʻena is Hanalei, the wettest and greenest part of the island, where mountain rains pour waterfalls over the dark green cliffs. Hanalei Bay, the largest on the island, is a favorite of yachtsmen. A variety of beautiful beaches ring the eastern coast of Kauaʻi, all the way down to the southernmost, and hottest, at Poʻipū. Off that southern tip is the Spouting Horn, where the tide sends up a fountain of water as it is forced through a funnel created by an old lava flow. Brennecke's Beach is a favorite of bodysurfers in search of the perfect wave.

When Captain James Cook first dropped anchor at Waimea in 1778, his visit did not get a royal reception because the local chiefs were apparently summering in cooler Wailua, on the island's east shore, at the time of his arrival. Nonetheless, Cook's discovery of the Islands marked the beginning of change. Wailua shortly became a busy port, and one of the most sought-after commodities was the island's fragrant sandalwood.

One of the more curious chapters in the history of Kauaʻi unfolded in 1816, when an industrious Russian agent concocted a scheme to help the Kauaʻi king, Kaumualiʻi, conquer all of the Islands. The scheme progressed only as far as the building of a fort near Waimea, a unique star-shaped structure of Russian design, executed by Hawaiian construction techniques.

A more direct and permanent impact came when the island's first sugar plantation was established at Kōloa in 1835. Laborers were imported from all over the world to tackle the backbreaking work in the sugar cane fields. The stir-fry of immigrants that arrived from Portugal, Japan, Puerto Rico, Norway, Germany, Spain, and the Philippines changed the character of the island's population.

In order to communicate and coexist, plantation immigrants developed "pidgin," a complicated mixture of English, Hawaiian, and other languages and dialects. Now the most common "ethnic" language in Hawaii, pidgin differs from island to island, often defying translation. Short-term visitors cannot hope to understand its subtle nuances or master its jaunty style. Gavan Daws, author of the Hawaiian history, *Shoal of Time,* suggests that pidgin is a sort of resistance movement—the local boys' last stand against the tourist invasion.

Times, and crops, have changed. Now the old sugar plantation at Kīlauea is devoted to raising prawns and guava. But this island has changed less rapidly than its neighbors. There are there are still many taro patches on Kauaʻi.

Taro, a low-growing, broad-leafed plant, is the source of *poi*—the sticky, pinkish-gray paste that has been a mainstay of the Hawaiian diet for centuries. Its starchy tuber, similar to a sweet potato, is baked in an *imu,* or underground oven, then pounded into a hard purple paste that can be reconstituted later to whatever thickness is desired.

Poi is eaten with the hand, by gracefully dipping the extended fingers. Depending on the thickness of the poi, it may be referred to as "two-finger" or "three-finger" poi. For Hawaiians, poi is more than mere sustenance. It should be eaten with a certain amount of ceremony. It is savored, and its character evaluated, with the same kind of attention that a glass of wine might merit.

Another remnant of Old Hawaii is a fragrant vine that grows especially well on Kauaʻi. Maile, dedicated to Laka, the goddess of dance, is the best known of six *lei*-making materials traditional to Old Hawaii. In Old Hawaii, a *lei* was made of vines and berries, and was used as an offering in religious dances. Flowers came much later, and the "traditional" *lei*-with-a-kiss greeting is actually a post-World War II innovation. A maile *lei* is a special honor, and the small-leafed *Maile lauliʻi* on Kauaʻi is especially fragrant. When *mokihana* berries from the mountains are twined with the maile, it becomes the most prized *lei* of all.

Seen from the air or on a map, Kauaʻi has the shape of an uncut gem. It has, in fact, that character. Much of Old Hawaii lingers on the lush, quiet "Garden Isle." Its remote valleys and rugged cliffs are still unsullied by roads. The peaceful beaches and poetic valleys of Kauaʻi, its colorful canyons and splashing waterfalls—all are sufficiently picture-perfect to convince the city-weary that dreams of escape to tropical paradise can indeed come true.

Hanalei Pier on Hanalei Bay

Waimea Canyon as seen from above the Mokuone Ridge

Waiʻaleʻale Crater, said to be the wettest place on earth

Majestic ʻŌpaekaʻa Falls

5,148-foot Mount Waiʻaleʻale on a very rare, clear day

Waimea Canyon, commonly called the Grand Canyon of the Pacific, is a 2,857-foot gorge cut into the Kōkeʻe Plateau.

Red-crested cardinal

Alakoko or Menehune Fishponds with Nāwiliwili Bay in the background

Tunnels Reef located on the north shore of Kaua'i

Cruise ship off the south coast near Hanapēpē

Ninini Point Light, on Nāwiliwili Bay

Footprints in golden sand at Kēʻē Beach, north shore of Kauaʻi

Waioli Huiʻia Church and Mission in Hanalei

Black-necked stilt in farmer's pond near Hanalei

Wailua Falls was the location for the opening scenes from the television program, "Fantasy Island."

Kēʻē Beach on the north shore

Taro farming in the Hanalei Valley

Water breaks over reef at Salt Pond State Park, south shore of Kaua'i

Tourist on Zodiac raft trip near the Nāpali Coast

Port Allen and town of Hanapēpē, south coast of Kaua'i

Gallery in Old Kōloa Town, Kōloa District

Kīlauea Lighthouse and Wildlife Refuge is a refuge for endangered sea birds.

'Eke Crater in the West Maui Mountains

Long, long ago, a cunning demigod named Māui lived on the slopes of Mount Haleakalā. Days on the island were shorter then, because the sun was so lazy it slept late and raced across the sky. In fact, the hours of sunlight were so few that Māui's mother, Hina, had trouble drying the soft *kapa* cloth she made from paper mulberry bark.

Māui solved the problem by waiting on the mountaintop one morning and snaring the sun as it rose over the crater's edge. Tying its rays with coconut fiber ropes, he held the sun hostage until it promised to slow down. Now the sun rises early and lingers elegantly over Haleakalā, lighting its yawning crater and giving it the right to be called "House of the Sun."

That crater is three thousand feet deep and twenty-one miles around, large enough to hold the island of Manhattan and silent as the face of the moon. Mark Twain, for whom the island of Maui was a favorite haunt, wrote of watching a sunrise there, "It was the sublimest spectacle I ever witnessed, and I think the memory of it will remain with me always."

Mount Haleakalā is the larger and younger of two volcanic mountains that fused, thousands of centuries ago, to create the island of Maui. West Maui rose from the ocean floor first and broke into several mountains. Haleakalā followed, rising 10,023 feet to form the island's larger eastern mass. The lava that bubbled and flowed between the two created the narrow, fertile isthmus that gives Maui its nickname, "the Valley Isle."

Hawaiians lived on this second largest of the Hawaiian Islands for centuries before the arrival of the first Europeans. The evidence in Hāna, at the eastern tip of Maui, suggests settlement there as early as A.D. 500. The island's character today is a captivating mixture of rural charm, work-a-day practicality, and laidback sophistication. It has become a favorite haven both for artists and for celebrities.

Wailuku, the county seat of Maui, is a low-key city with a healthy measure of nineteenth-century charm. Its old stone Ka'ahumanu Church, which was named for Kamehameha's favorite wife, stands as a reminder of the eagerness with which Hawaiian royalty embraced missionary Christianity.

A bloody battle, fought in the Iao Valley, three miles inland from Wailuku, marked Maui's first step into the modern world. There, in 1790, Kamehameha the Great, on his way to uniting the Islands under one rule, won the decisive victory over his rival chiefs on Maui. Forced into the narrow, steep-walled valley, the Maui warriors fought against Kamehameha's newly acquired English cannon until, by some accounts, Iao Stream was so full of bodies that the water was unable to flow. Iao Valley, whose name means "asking for clouds," is now a state park. At its center is the curious, 2,350-foot cinder-cone pinnacle that is known as Iao Needle.

Wailuku's sister city, Kahului, is the commercial center of the island. After World War II, Harry and Frank Baldwin tried to make it a "dream city" for sugar and pineapple workers, whose living accommodations during the height of the plantation era had been less than desirable. Cane grew in Old Hawaii, but it took American entrepreneurs to see its commercial potential. Pineapple, so much a part of the island's image today, was not introduced until 1820 and did not become a big export until the twentieth century.

After the middle of the nineteenth century, West Maui belonged to the sugar plantation owners. The thousands of laborers they imported from China, Japan, and Portugal to work the cane fields created the island's present racial mix. Maui's fields still yield one-fourth of Hawaii's annual sugar crop, as well as half its pineapple.

South across the rich agricultural valley, by way of a highway that cuts through placid green countryside and passes between red-soiled fields striped with silver-green pineapple plants, is the blue curve of Mā'alaea Bay. The bay is the spawning grounds for the humpback whales that migrate from Alaska to play all winter in the warmer waters off Maui. During the winter months, Maui is a prime research center for the study of whale behavior.

Spectacular beaches and grand ocean views line the road from Mā'alaea Bay to Lahaina. Between, at Olowalu, is one of the Islands' best petroglyph sites. Similar collections of symbols, stick people, and animals have been found scratched on rock surfaces in out-of-the-way places on every island. Writer/art critic John Charlot suggests that the Hawaiians' deep respect for the integrity of nature caused them to keep their additions to it unobtrusive. These simple drawings—often hidden in brush, in caves, or where the rising tide would cover them—may have been records of important events or aids to telling stories. Now, the story-tellers are gone, and the petroglyphs' meanings are a mystery.

The whales who bear their young in Mā'alaea Bay can now swim on with their calves—undisturbed—to Lahaina, the port that was brought to life in the nineteenth century by the quest for their ancestors' bones and blubber. Lahaina's glory-days began in 1819, when King Liholiho, eldest son of Kamehameha the Great, made it the capital of his kingdom. The first American whaling ships made port a few years later. The dusty, grass-hut village quickly became a favorite port of call. Whalers favored the offshore waters, called the "Lahaina Roads," since they are sheltered by the smaller islands of Lānaʻi and Molokaʻi and provide safe harbor in any weather. For the next two decades, masts filled the harbor, and thousands of sailors frequented the bars on Front Street. One who jumped ship there was Herman Melville, author of the whaling saga, *Moby Dick.*

The missionaries, who arrived shortly after the whalers, worked arduously to save the souls of the locals. Kamehameha's second wife, Keopuolani, supported and encouraged the missionaries in their endeavors. Opened in 1831, Lahaina Luna Seminary became the oldest American high school west of the Rockies. During the raucous days of the California Gold Rush, many young men were sent there from the West Coast to receive a proper education. Among the Hawaiians educated there was David Malo, a Native scholar so well respected that one of Maui's favorite annual celebrations is David Malo Day.

In 1845, the kingdom moved to Oʻahu, and shortly after, the whaling trade declined. Lahaina became again a sleepy town until 1962, when it was made a National Historic District and restoration was begun. Now behind Front Street's nineteenth-century, movie-set charm are galleries, gourmet restaurants, and a lively night-life. Where sailors once thronged, tourists with ice-cream cones now stroll, peering in shop windows, watching a parrot-trainer put on a colorful sidewalk show, or aiming for the shade of the famous—and enormous—century-old banyon tree.

Tourists now sun on the island's best beaches. Growing strings of destination resorts line the golden sands of Kāʻanapali, west beyond Lahaina, and Kīhei, east of Māʻalaea Bay.

East Maui, dominated by the bulk of Haleakalā, is more rural than the island's western side. Between the national park, encompassing Haleakalā's crater, and the central valley is "Upcountry"— quiet country towns, wooded farms, and ranches where horses graze and fields sprout volunteer crops of giant cacti. It is the land of the "paniolos," cowboys whose name comes from Hawaiian mispronunciation of *español.* Upcountry ranches command views that make it easy to understand why locals unabashedly contend: *Maui nō ka ʻoi*—Maui is the best. From the slope of Haleakalā, the valley rolls out below, green and fertile, bound on either edge by crescents of brilliant blue and caught up on the other side by the richly shadowed mountains of West Maui.

A *Kamaʻāina,* an old-timer, might contend that Upcountry is the heart of Maui. Beyond the town of Pukalani, "Hole in the Heavens," is the Kula district. The volcanic soil is rich, and all kinds of fruits and vegetables thrive. One unique crop is protea, an intriguing tropical flower which growers hope to market worldwide.

Another botanical curiosity, silversword, grows exclusively on the slopes of Haleakalā. This striking, ball-shaped plant is covered with thousands of daggerlike, silver-green leaves and, before it dies, produces a single stem of yellow and purple florets. It can grow to eight feet tall and may live as long as twenty years.

Below Pukalani, toward the coast, is sugar country. But a newer industry has given life to Pāʻia, where Samuel Alexander and Henry Baldwin built their sugar plantation in 1870. Windsurfers have discovered Hoʻokipa Beach and claim it is the "windsurfing capital of the world." This, plus the fact that it is the gateway on the popular road to Hāna, has given this town a hip new style.

The "heavenly" road to Hāna, which begins at Pāʻia and wanders along East Maui's north shore, is a winding idyl into Hawaii's past. The narrow road passes through lush forests of exotic trees; provides glimpses of coastal villages with stone walls and taro patches which have looked the same for centuries; snakes over charming, one-lane bridges; and passes splashing waterfalls. The air is sweet; the scenery, tranquil and unbelievably picturesque. But the road is no secret. Choose the wrong hour on a weekend, and you may travel its fifty-two miles bumper-to-bumper.

The Hāna road was an engineering triumph during an era when enthusiastic pioneers were willing to try anything; once, there was even a rubber plantation on this coast. Under optimum conditions, it takes almost three hours to navigate its 617 curves and 56 one-lane bridges. Its destination, the remote and ancient village where Kamehameha the Great's favorite wife, Kaʻahumanu, was born, has now become a celebrity hide-out.

Beyond Hāna, the road gets rougher, and the present indeed falls away. Charles Lindberg, the legendary aviator, found the solitude he craved in Kapahulu, where waterfalls splash into green valleys and sunrise lights both sides of the sky. Dying of cancer in a New York hospital in 1974, Lindberg insisted on being flown back to the place he loved most in all the world. "I would rather live one day in Maui," he said, "than a month in New York."

Right: Weeping Wall in West Maui Mountains

Above: Giant bronze Buddha at the Jodo Mission in Lahaina
Left: Water flower near Hāna

Above: ʻOheʻo Gulch, commonly called the "Seven Sacred Pools"
Right: Windsurfing on the north shore of Maui

Windsurfing at Hoʻokipa Beach, north coast of Maui

People gather from all over the world to windsurf the northern coast of Maui.

Silversword on south slope of Haleakalā Crater

Pineapple harvesting on western slope of West Maui Mountains

Kā'anapali Beach, claimed by many to be one of the most beautiful beaches in the world

The old whaling town of Lahaina at sunset

Hobi Cat Race in a Maui channel

Popular sport of canoe racing off Papawai Point

Lahaina Harbor

Cinder cones in Haleakalā Crater

West Maui Mountains

Honokalā Point on the north coast of Maui

Nene, Hawaiian geese, near the Haleakalā Crater in Haleakalā National Park

Ancient fishing village and *Heiau,* "Hawaiian temple," on the south coast

Kāʻanapali Beach from above Lahaina

'Ālau Island just off the town of Hāna

Iao Needle in the Iao Valley

Lahaina Harbor

Molokini Islet off the southern coast of Maui

Kula Ulupalakua Ranch area on the southwestern slope of Haleakalā

Southern slope of Haleakalā

Colorful cinder cones at the bottom of Haleakalā Crater from observatory

Above: The *Carthaginian II,* a reproduction of a whaling ship once stationed in Lahaina, is moored in Lahaina Harbor.
Right: Beach at Puamana State Park

When the outside world and the Hawaiian Islands discovered each other two centuries ago, their meeting released a tidal wave of change. The small island of O'ahu, with its perfect natural harbor, took the wave full force. Eighty percent of Hawaii's total population now lives on O'ahu, which is Hawaii's third-largest island and constitutes only ten percent of its land. Honolulu has become a true American metropolis—with a few differences. What other state capital has *lei* stands at its airport, double rainbows over its freeways, and an authentic royal palace in midtown?

Two centuries ago, O'ahu was as quiet and rural as the other Hawaiian Islands. Maui and the Big Island were, in fact, greater centers of power. Ordinary Hawaiians grew taro, breadfruit, and sugar cane in O'ahu's rich valleys and caught the fish that teemed off its shores. The only interruptions to the gentle rhythm of life were squabbles between rival local chiefs.

To relax, the chiefs and other *ali'i*, the privileged nobility, liked to retreat to a fishing village in a swampy area called Waikīkī, or "Spouting Water." Bordering the swamp was a long curve of beautiful white-sand beach, palm-shaded and coral-protected, that was rich with fish and had perfect surfing waves. There, the tall, powerfully built *ali'i* rode the waves nobly on eighteen-foot-long, fifty-pound planks of koa wood.

Down the coast from the Waikīkī swamp was another collection of fishing shacks clustered around a peaceful basin of water called Honolulu, or "Sheltered Bay." The stage was set, but all the major players had not yet arrived.

Captain James Cook did not stop on O'ahu. But in 1792, an English sea captain named William Brown accidentally found his way through a narrow channel and into a perfect anchorage on O'ahu's south shore. It was, he reported, "a small but commodious basin with regular soundings from seven to three fathoms, clear and good bottom, where a few vessels may ride with the greatest safety." He called it "Fair Haven."

Once discovered, "Fair Haven," best known by its Hawaiian name of Honolulu, became a magnet for vessels sailing from England or America to Chinese ports. Those ships carried goods the Hawaiians had never seen, but quickly knew they wanted. Little as they knew of possessions and trade, it did not take them long to catch on. The inland valleys emptied as it became obvious that the excitement—and the profit—now centered on the wharf. Honolulu eventually became the economic focal point for all the Islands and the site of their royal capital.

Captain Brown, the discoverer, was an early casualty of island politics. He was killed during a 1795 stopover, when O'ahu's ruling chief, Kalanikupule, was intent on acquiring British guns. The guns were to use against Kamehameha, the powerful chief from the Big Island who had already conquered Maui and would eventually bring all the Islands under his power. Kamehameha invaded and conquered O'ahu, driving Kalanikupule's warriors into the Nu'uanu Valley and over its sheer twelve-hundred-foot *pali* (cliff), in a dramatic final defeat. Kalanikupule himself later became a human sacrifice to Kamehameha's battle god, Kukailimoku.

Kamehameha proved to be the right man for the times. Both resourceful and shrewd, he managed to get what he needed from the foreigners while keeping them at bay. His successors were less adept, and over the years, the power of the monarchy eroded in the face of foreign economic interests.

Kukailimoku, the fierce, feathered idol Kamehameha carried into battle, now stares benignly from a case in Honolulu's Bishop Museum. Other memories of Old Hawaii are also relegated to those shelves—graceful hooks carved of bone that once lured great fish from the sea; koa-wood *calabashes,* community food bowls that gleam from the strokes of many fingers; intricately patterned swaths of *kapa,* the soft bark-cloth that few remember how to make.

Exposure to the ways of the *haole* (white man) unpinned the basic structure of Hawaiian life. Natives watched foreigners break the sacred *kapus* with no ill effects and began to doubt the rules by which they had lived for centuries. To Hawaiians, *haole* concepts of land ownership, money, and trade were altogether new, and often confusing. The Old Hawaiian gods began to fade from the stage, making room for the next major players—the missionaries and the entrepreneurs.

Hawaiians called the first missionaries, who arrived in 1919, "long necks" because of their high collars. In their zeal to teach, clothe, and "civilize," these stiff New Englanders repressed much that was Hawaiian. But it is to their credit that the Hawaiian language can now be written, and that music has become one of the Hawaiian's great joys. (Hymn-singing was a revelation to the Hawaiians. The only music they had known prior to the arrival of the missionaries was drums and chanting). The big, coral-block Kawaiahao Church they built in downtown Honolulu became an important Hawaiian gathering place.

It was the sons of the missionaries who first saw the tremendous economic potential in O'ahu's fertile volcanic soil and busy harbor. Other venturesome American entrepreneurs followed, and the mid-nineteenth century became the era of pineapple and sugar cane. For this part of the drama, the script called for a large cast.

Left: City of Honolulu from Ko'olau Range

To take the vast plantations to their maximum production, the owners imported cheap labor from all over the world. Japanese, Chinese, Portuguese, and Filipinos flooded in to swell the island's population and, eventually, change its face. For these immigrant laborers, the work was hard, and life was lonely and sometimes confusing. But for their children, Hawaii was the land of opportunity. Today, their descendents make its laws, manage its finances, and run its corporations.

As more and more ships docked in Honolulu, adventurous travelers discovered the pleasures of Waikīkī beach. By the late 1800s, hardy tourists like writer Robert Louis Stevenson were taking a mule-drawn omnibus from Honolulu to the shore's first "family resort," grandly dubbed the Sans Souci. In 1901, the elegant Moana became the first real hotel on the beach. The tourist business looked promising, and in 1922 the swamp was drained.

With the opening of the chic pink Royal Hawaiian in 1927, the era of the grand Hawaiian cruise vacation began. When the elegant ships steamed into port, locals crowded the dock, and the Royal Band stood near the brand new, ten-story-tall Aloha Tower to play the sweet, languid strains of "Aloha O'i." For three decades more, an air of genteel exclusivity prevailed. Then came statehood, equity capitol, and jet travel, and Waikīkī grew by quantum leaps. Today, a mass of high-rise hotels has grown from the swamp, and the royal surfing beach has become a glitzy international playground. In less than a quarter of a decade, the transformation has been drastic. But the most important elements remain unchanged. The perfect waves roll in all day, and at evening the sun still sinks gloriously into the sea.

The essence of Hawaii's charisma is, after all, its great natural beauty. Away from the hustle and glitter of Honolulu and Waikīkī, that fact is easier to appreciate. It does not take long to escape to other parts of O'ahu; to ignore the remainder of this island is to miss an important part of its character.

East, beyond the postcard-familiar shape of Diamond Head (named by British seamen who mistook its deposits of calcite for something more valuable) are the beautiful blue arc of Hanauma Bay, a snorkeler's paradise, and the land bulge called Koko Head, another place where the fire goddess, Pele, was frustrated in her search for a suitable home. On the eastern tip of land called Makapu'u, "Bulging Eye," twelve-foot waves challenge expert body-surfers. All along the coast, where blue waves splash on black lava rock, are spectacular ocean views.

The gentle slopes of the Ko'olau Mountains run the length of eastern O'ahu, forming a backdrop for Honolulu and dividing it

from the island's eastern, or windward, side. Warm trade winds always lap the windward coast, reaching gale force on the Pali between. Less than half an hour across the Pali Highway from Honolulu, windward O'ahu is worlds away in spirit.

In Kailua Beach Park, directly across the Pali Highway from Honolulu, a mass of multicolored sails mark the best windsurfing beach in the state. Inland from the quiet town of Kailua is Mount Olomana, the 1,643-foot peak believed to be the volcanic origin of O'ahu. Up the coast beyond Kāne'ohe, the largest population center on the windward side, are little towns like Waiāhole and Waikāne, where fruit stands line the roads and the spirit of rural, old-time O'ahu can still be felt.

In winter, twenty-five-foot waves thunder in at Waimea Bay, 'Ehukai, Sunset, and Banzai Pipeline, the world-famous surfing beaches along O'ahu's north shore. The lure of the sport has lent new character to the little town of Hale'iwa. People of all ages, colors and persuasions congregate at its country store for the island's best "shave ice," the concoction that is Hawaii's answer to the ice-cream cone.

Pineapple fields still carpet central O'ahu, an area where remnants of Old Hawaii remain. Near Wahiawā, a place of great spiritual importance to early Hawaiians, it is possible to see the healing stones, whose vibrations were said to cure maladies, and the royal birthing stones, where ali'i went to deliver each royal keiki (child), hiding the pico, (umbilical cord) in a special crevice to assure the child's future happiness.

One part of O'ahu still belongs, both spiritually and culturally, to the ethnic Hawaiians. It is the island's northwest, or leeward, coast. Defined by the rugged Wai'anae Mountains, the area has retained a character very much its own. It is not many miles, or minutes, from the southern tip of O'ahu to the leeward shore. But three other worlds—Waikīkī, Honolulu, and Pearl Harbor—lie between.

That is what has happened on O'ahu—many different worlds have learned to coexist gracefully in very little space. Many different players have shared the stage.

Behind the establishment of Honolulu's Bishop Museum is a true love story that reads like a parable. A century and a half ago, Bernice Pauahi, a genuine Hawaiian princess and the last of Kamehameha's line, fell in love with Charles Reed Bishop, a successful haole businessman. She broke her childhood betrothal and defied her family's wishes in order to marry him. She gave up her past to embrace Hawaii's new reality. He built a museum in her memory to preserve her heritage.

Coral reefs in Hanauma Bay Beach Park

Waikīkī Beach

Diamond Head with Waikīkī Beach and Honolulu in background

Bon Odori Festival Parade down Kalākaua Avenue

Mōkapu Peninsula with Mōkapu Point and Pyramid Rock, east or windward side of the island of Oʻahu.

Tourist snorkeling in Kāneʻohe Bay

Tourists gather when a school of fish is found.

Mokoli'i Islet known to many by its more popular name of Chinaman's Hat

Hanauma Bay, very popular snorkeling location because of protected fish population

On the island of Oʻahu, the most famous beach of all—Waikīkī

Tropical fish can be seen from almost all of Hawaii's beaches.

Koʻolau Mountain Range

Above: Sunset dinner cruise off Diamond Head
Right: Diamond Head Lighthouse located at the base of Diamond Head Crater

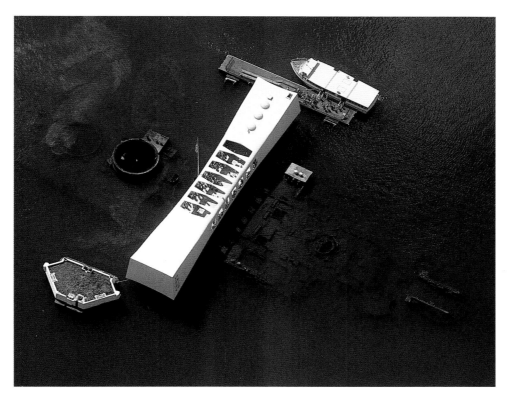

Above: Arizona Memorial in Pearl Harbor
Left: Ala Moana Beach Park, Waikīkī, and Diamond Head

Above: Shipwrecks in Pearl Harbor
Right: Polynesian dancers performing at the Polynesian Cultural Center

Waikīkī Beach looking toward Diamond Head

Puʻu Kānehoalani Peak near Kāneʻohe Bay

ʻIolani Palace in downtown Honolulu

Catamaran cruising off Waikīkī

Byodo-in-Temple at the Valley of the Temples near Kāneʻohe is a replica of a 900-year-old Japanese temple.

Makapu'u Point Lighthouse

Puʻu Kānehoalani Peak from across Kāneʻohe Bay

Cruise ship in Honolulu Harbor getting ready to sail

Busy evening on Kalākaua Avenue

Sacred Falls on the windward side of island

Koko Crater on the windward coast

Puʻuōʻō Volcano Vent in Hawaii Volcanoes National Park

In Old Hawaii mythology, the Earth Mother and the Sky Father had two beautiful daughters who were bitter rivals. They were Pele, the keeper of fire, and Na Maka o Kahaʻi, who ruled the sea. When Pele went in search of a home, her spiteful older sister followed, spoiling each site she chose. Pele fled from island to island, until finally, on the last and largest, she found a place her fires could burn. There she settled, and lives today, in the firepit of Kīlauea.

In the ancient myth was the essence of geologic truth. The volcanic mountains which created the Hawaiian Islands rose from the sea in succession, from northwest to southeast. On Hawaii, the youngest island, fire and water are still battling to shape the land. Mauna Loa is the world's largest active volcano, and Kīlauea, the world's liveliest.

So Pele, a powerful goddess with a fiery temper, still periodically spews lava from her home into the sea, and believers still pay her proper respect. Stone cairns and offerings of flower crowns, anthurium bouquets, and bottles of gin can still be seen at the end of lava flows and at craters' rims.

Pele's home is now the center of Hawaii Volcanoes National Park, which reaches inland to Mauna Loa and southeast to the sea. Visitors can drive around the rim of Kīlauea, walk through a lava tube, and wonder at the unearthly expanse of lava-covered desolation. Here and there, tiny, tenacious red-flowered bushes confirm that nothing in these Islands remains lifeless for long.

It is possible to hike south on "Desolation Trail" and, if conditions are right, watch the steam rise as boiling lava rolls slowly into the sea. In Hawaii, even the volcanoes are gentle, rarely erupting violently. Rather, Pele's caldrons boil, and lava oozes out slowly, taking a predictable course. In the destruction is also creation, as the new layers of lava, over time, become rich new land.

All this volcanic action produces some curiosities. Hawaii has not only beautiful, white-sand beaches, but a few lava-sand beaches that are black, and even one that is green. The green sand, the result of a deposit of olivine in the lava flow, is at Ka Lae, South Point, which is the southernmost point in the United States. It is also the place where the earliest Polynesian explorers probably made their first landfall, perhaps as early as A.D. 150.

To locals, Hawaii is always "Big Island." It is, indeed, twice as big as Maui, Oʻahu, Kauaʻi, and Molokaʻi combined, and not yet through growing. Its land surface is ninety-three miles wide and ninety-six miles long, but there is more to its size if you consider its underwater bulk. Two massive shield volcanoes form its core. If the sea were drained to reveal their total stature, they would dwarf the other mountains in the world. Mauna Kea rises 13,667 feet, and Mauna Loa, 13,769 feet, above sea level. But the full height of each mountain, measured from the ocean floor, is nearly thirty thousand feet.

Volcanic soil and mountain air make the Kona area the source of a unique crop. America's only coffee plantations are on the Kona slopes of Mauna Kea. There is more demand for the beans, which make a uniquely smooth-flavored brew, than can be supplied.

Considering that the Big Island's land surface is smaller than the state of Vermont, the contrasts it contains are amazing. The main highway around the island, which could be driven (but not appreciated) in six hours, passes cane fields, orchid farms, macadamia nut orchards, lava desolation, coffee plantations, destination resorts, and cattle ranches in bewilderingly rapid succession. Rain forest and desert, lava fields and lush farmland virtually rub shoulders; the perpetually sunny Kona coast gets only fifteen inches of rain a year, while verdant Hilo across the island receives nearly ten times that much. When it is 80° in Kona, there is snow for skiing thirty miles away, on Mauna Kea's slopes.

Big Island's two major cities, directly across the island from one another, are as different as their climates. Hilo, the island's major population center, is a sleepy, rain-drenched country town, friendly and unpretentious. It is both stubbornly old-fashioned and uncommercial, and its lack of "city-slick" is the essence of its charm. Tourist entertainments are as simple as standing at the Suisan fishmarket in the chilly dawn, coffee in hand, to watch the locals present the morning's catch; strolling through beautifully manicured Liliʻuokalani Park; or watching the stars wink on at nightfall above the graceful crescent of Hilo Bay.

Kailua/Kona, on the western coast, has the sun and the sunset—and the tourists' interests at heart. Inland it is quiet, but the harbor pulses with life. Cruise boats put out daily into waters that are a sport fisherman's paradise. ʻAhi, mahimahi, billfish, and spearfish abound; and fishermen boast of thousand-pound catches. The waterfront and side streets are crowded with shops, begging to be browsed. When daylight fades, long Hawaiian canoes put out into the sunset, tourists crowd the many restaurants, and the streetlights twinkle like an elegant carnival.

Between these two harbors, around the southern periphery of the island, are small towns with pristine white churches and spreading jacaranda trees, and an atmosphere little changed in four decades. Children go barefoot to school, healthfood stores sit next to tattoo parlors, and—along with pizza and videos—country groceries sell plastic-bagged poi.

The Kona Coast is rich in history. South of Kailua, beyond Kealakekua Bay, is a piece of Old Hawaii which has been impeccably restored. It is Pu'uhonua O Hōnaunau, the City of Refuge. There were other such sanctuaries, but this was the largest in the Islands. It was a haven for defeated warriors, *kapu* breakers, and women and children in time of war.

If wrongdoers were able to escape and swim the bay to this finger of land, the *kahuna* was obliged to perform the rituals that absolved them of their crimes. Its temple stands among the tall, royal palms that marked its location, protected by a semi-circle of carved gods. The only sounds are the click of palm fronds in the gentle breeze and the irreverent chatter of mynah birds. Black lava, white coral, and the browns and grays of dried grass and weathered wood create a sharp contrast to the vibrant blue of sky and sea. The solitude of Pu'uhonua O Hōnaunau speaks eloquently of the past, and visitors hush to listen

Kona was also the land of Lono, the Hawaiian god of fertility. The Makahiki Festival in Lono's honor was underway when Captain James Cook, the first white man to land in the Islands, anchored in Kealakekua Bay in 1778. The Hawaiians mistook Cook for Lono, who was supposed to be tall and fair and arrive waving white banners. They welcomed Cook and his men with feasting and generosity, never doubting his godliness until he departed, then returned to the harbor to make ship repairs. Tragic misunderstandings ensued, and the great English seaman was slain in the harbor during a scuffle over a canoe.

European discovery became a catalyst at a crucial juncture in local Island history. When Cook arrived, the Islands were divided among feuding rival kings. A young chief from Kohala was just beginning to plan the campaign that would eventually bring all the Islands under his rule. Europeans who met Kamehameha noted his obvious intelligence and charisma, but remarked on his fierce countenance. Kamehameha, in turn, took note of the foreigners' advantages, iron and firearms, and made use of them in his conquests. Later, that same pragmatism kept the Islands intact under his rule, as more and more English and American ships arrived.

In the decade after Cook's arrival, Kamehameha conquered Maui, Lāna'i and Moloka'i. But he could not overcome his rival and cousin, Keōua, in the southeastern part of his own island of Hawaii. The island's most powerful *kahuna* advised him to build a mighty *heiau,* or temple, to his fierce war god, Kuka'ilimoku. It was to be in Pu'ukoholā, the "hill of the whale," on the Kohala coast north of Kailua, an arid region that looks very much like the mainland's southwest.

Thousands of workers labored to complete the structure, carrying all the lava boulders from thirty miles away. When Keōua marshalled an army to stop the process, the volcano suddenly erupted, and a third of his men were lost.

Their footprints can still be seen encased in the lava on a trail in Hawaii Volcanoes National Park. Keōua accepted the inevitable, came to the *heiau*'s dedication, was slain on arrival, and became its first human sacrifice. The shell of the structure remains today, an ominous curve of black against the golden dried grass, under the clear, bright-blue Kona sky.

Pu'ukoholā commands a breathtaking view out to sea and down the coast. On the sweep of coast to its south are the glorious, white-sand beaches of 'Anaeho'omalu Bay, now the center of a string of elegant tourist resorts.

Hāmākua, the northeast portion of Hawaii, is the land of cane fields and cowboys. The Parker Ranch, which surrounds Waimea, grew from two acres given by King Kamehameha to a resourceful New Englander named John Palmer Parker in return for solving a problem. Domestic animals the king had received as gifts from visiting foreigners had been allowed to run loose and multiply. Within a few years, wild cattle, sheep, and goats were trampling the island's unfenced farmland, gnawing trees, and being a general nuisance. Parker corralled the cattle, and over time, the two acres he was given as a reward grew into what is probably the largest privately owned ranch in the United States, a spread that is desert-like on one side and bordered by rain forest on the other.

Beyond the Parker ranch, Hāmākua is a dramatically rugged coast of deep green valleys and splashing waterfalls. It is sugar country, with tiny, rural towns where the descendents of the early plantations' Scottish, Japanese, Filipino, and Portuguese laborers, who were imported at the end of the last century, still live quietly. Sugar's place in the economy is shrinking, and a newer crop from Australia—macadamia nuts—is a possible substitute.

Around Hilo, where everything blooms in such mad profusion, another crop thrives. This area is the premier source of orchids on the Islands. These exotic symbols of the tropics come in all colors, sizes, and shapes, on long stems loaded with blooms. For that reason, Hawaii is sometimes called "the Orchid Isle."

"Volcano Island" is another popular nickname. The variety on the island suggests a dozen more that would also fit.

But "Big Island" is the name that seems most right for this youngest of the Islands. It is the handsome, hulking, good-natured adolescent of the Island family, unaware of its own strength, full of promise, and still growing.

Right: New life in Lava, Hawaii Volcanoes National Park

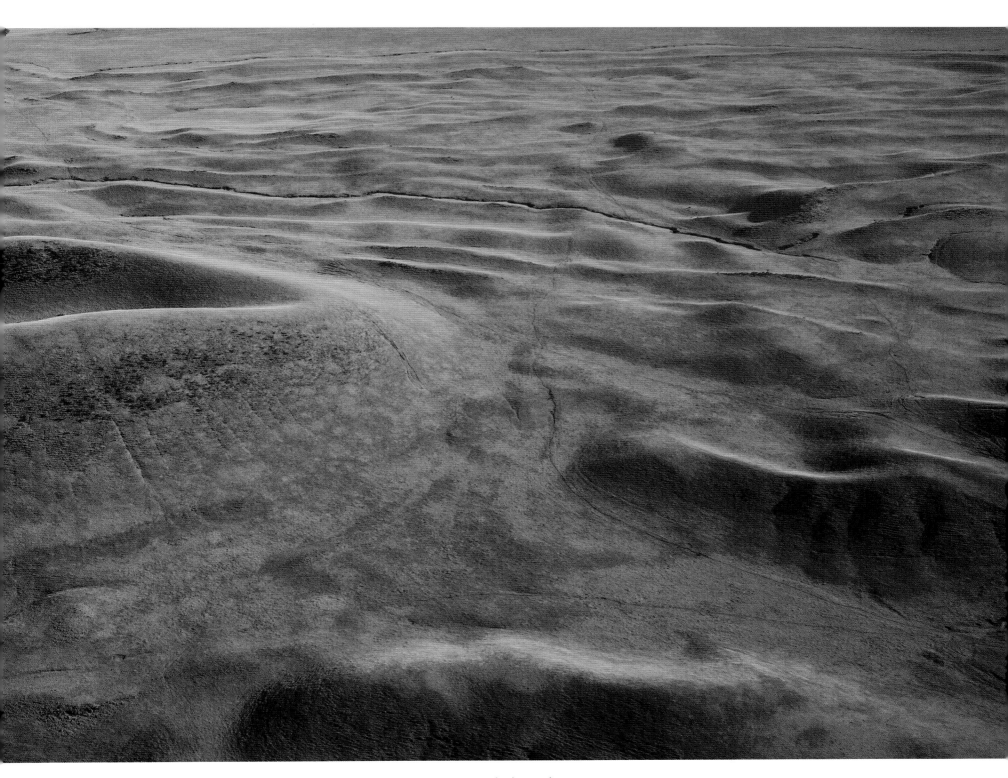

Cinder cones on south slope of Mauna Kea

Puʻuhonua o Hōnaunau, commonly called the City of Refuge

High surf at Laupāhoehoe Point

Wooden *kii* images guard the reconstruction of Haleo-Keawe Temple at the City of Refuge National Park.

Large gathering of Royal Poinciana

Waterfalls in Waimanu Valley on the Hāmākua Coast

Small peaceful waterfall on the Hāmākua Coast

Lava flows entering the sea near Waha'ula in Hawaii Volcanoes National Park

The summit of Mauna Loa Volcano at 13,677 feet

Kiʻilae Bay and the City of Refuge

Picturesque St. Peter's Catholic Church in South Kona

Above: Kealakekua Bay and Captain Cook Memorial, where Captain Cook was killed in 1779 during altercation with locals
Right: Tropical jungle on the Hāmākua Coast

Above: Coral reef from two hundred feet in the air
Left: Some locals call it *melia;* others, *plumeria.*

Above: Petroglyphs carved in rock at the Hyatt Regency Waikoloa
Right: Puʻukohola Heiau on the Kawaihae Coast

'Akaka Falls is one of the most famous points of interest in Hawaii.

City of Hilo, second-largest city in the Hawaiian Islands

Lava pond in Hawaii Volcanoes National Park

Fresh hot lava from flow near Kalapana

Above: Start of Hawaiian International Billfish Tournament held each year in late July and early August
Right: Hāmākua Coast looking toward Waipiʻo Valley

Hawaiians used a story to explain the emergence of their islands from the sea. The legend goes something like this: the mischievous demigod Māui, out fishing one day with his more serious and productive brothers, was determined to catch the biggest fish. He gave his hook a mighty toss, only to have it snag in the ocean floor. As he struggled to pull it up, he cautioned his brothers not to look. He was planning to pull up a mighty piece of land, but one of them sneaked a glance. The land shattered, and the Islands were formed.

Hawaii did, in truth, rise dramatically from the depths of the ocean, but the process took millions of years. It began during the mid-Tertiary Period, between twenty-five and forty million years ago. Volcanic vents under the floor of the Pacific forced hot magma through weak spots in the shifting Pacific plate. A series of volcanic mountains rose up in a curve, northwest to southeast, across the ocean floor. One after another, their peaks reached the surface of the ocean, spewing hot lava to be cooled and carved by the wind and waves. These violently sculpted mountaintops became the Hawaiian Archipelago.

The Hawaiian Archipelago contains, in all, 132 islands, shoals, atolls, and reefs. It arcs five hundred miles across the central Pacific Ocean, from tiny Kure Atoll, northwest of Midway, to Lō'ihi, an undersea mountain southeast of the Big Island that may someday emerge from the water's depths and become a new Hawaiian Island.

Over millions of years, as new islands grew, older and smaller islands aged, crumbled, and disappeared. Most familiar to us now are the archipelago's youngest members. The eight largest are, from northwest to southeast, Ni'ihau, Kaua'i, O'ahu, Moloka'i, Lāna'i, Maui, Kaho'olawe, and Hawaii.

An extraordinary natural harbor has made O'ahu the commercial heart of the group, and the world's playground. Once, O'ahu was synonymous with Hawaii, but now Maui, Hawaii, and Kaua'i are developing their own reputations, at least among the *akamai* (smart) vacationers. The three smallest of the eight islands are quieter family members who continue to hover, shyly, around the party's periphery.

The flavor of Old Hawaii pervades quiet, rural Moloka'i, the fifth-largest Hawaiian Island. It has been little touched by tourism, despite being promoted, quite rightly, as "The Friendly Isle." Of its sixty-five hundred residents, more than half are Hawaiian.

Moloka'i is a slipper-shaped strip of land formed by three volcanoes. Though barely thirty-seven miles long and less than ten miles wide, it has more than its share of spectacular scenery.

The largest white-sand beach on the Islands, Pāpōhaku Beach graces its western shore. In Hālawa Valley is Kahiwa Falls, Hawaii's largest waterfall, a thundering seventeen hundred feet tall. Moa'ula Falls, not as tall, is reputedly the home of a *mo'o,* a water being that is in the form of a giant dragon. Swimmers are advised to toss in a leaf before entering its pool—and to retreat hastily if the leaf disappears.

The drive from Kaunakakai, the center of trade on Moloka'i, to the lush Hālawa Valley is a winding, bumpy, breathtakingly beautiful two-hour trip. Kaunakakai, a sleepy country town with a wide main street, wooden buildings, and false storefronts, has a population of only about a thousand. Competition from the Philippines and Taiwan has shut down the pineapple business that once fueled this island's economy. Now the land is given primarily to cattle ranching.

The island's history is long. In the now-deserted Hālawa Valley, evidence has been found of human settlement as early as A.D. 650. Sheltered in the three-thousand-foot-deep valley is the oldest *heiau,* or temple, in the Islands, a massive lava-rock structure built in the thirteenth century as a temple for human sacrifice. Moloka'i was renowned among the Islands as the home of powerful *kahunas,* or priests. Some were wise seers and healers; others were fearful sorcerers.

At Pu'u-o-Hoku, the "Hill of the Stars" Ranch at the southeast end of the island, is a sacred grove of silvery-leafed kukui trees which once circled the home of a Kalanikāula, a great *kahuna.* Hawaiian laborers refused to clear the land for Del Monte, and the pineapples planted there reportedly wilted.

Before the Europeans came, Hawaiian settlements filled the Hālawa Valley and clustered along the southern coast. Those early Hawaiians tended taro fields and grew fish in the stone-ringed ponds along the southern shore. Built during the fifteenth century, the ponds had walls of coral and basalt, with wooden gratings through which small fish could swim, but from which the fattened fish could not escape. Now the state of Hawaii is investigating new ways to bolster the sagging economy of Moloka'i, and the ancient fishponds have become laboratories for developing a native seaweed culture.

During the nineteenth century, after Hawaiian rulers discovered the trade value of sandalwood, all the fragrant sandalwood trees from the island's central forests were logged for eventual sale to the Orient. Some say the older laborers cut down all the saplings to save later generations from the slave conditions they suffered in harvesting the wood.

Left: Kona sunset

The highest sea cliffs in the world make the northern shore of Moloka'i a fortress. Jutting out from that rugged, remote coast is a tiny peninsula called Makanalua, "The Given Grave." There, beginning in 1866, victims of Hansen's Disease, called leprosy, were brought by government skiffs and abandoned to die. Father Damien Joseph de Veuster, the young Belgian missionary who arrived in 1873 and gave his life to creating a community for these outcasts, is one of Hawaii's most beloved heroes.

Over the years, writers like Robert Louis Stevenson, Jack London, and James A. Michener have contributed to making the community of Kalaupapa famous. Although medical science has brought the disease under control, about a hundred residents still choose to live in Kalaupapa, a childless community with little future. No roads lead there. Tourists must travel by plane or mule to see Father Damien's small, white church standing tall and proud among the palms on its remote shore.

Lāna'i, the small, pear-shaped island south of Moloka'i, was not settled until about A.D. 1400, because Hawaiians believed it was a gathering place for evil spirits. According to legend, the problem was resolved when a Maui king exiled his mischievous son, Kaulula'au, to the deserted island to teach him a lesson. The crafty boy tracked down and disposed of every ghost and became a hero for making the island habitable.

A single crater created this rocky, red-soiled island. During the late eighteenth century, the island was fought over by many chieftains. Kamehameha the Great was fond of Lāna'i and, after conquering the island in 1795, made his summer home at Kaunolū Bay on the island's southwestern cape, where the fishing was good. The island's trademark Norfolk pines grew from seeds planted early in the twentieth century by George C. Munro, a New Zealander who managed the Lāna'i Ranch.

Lāna'i City was established in 1924 to house the 150 foreign laborers Jim Dole had imported to work in his pineapple fields. Today, most of the island belongs to Castle & Cooke, the company that now owns Dole, and most of the approximately two thousand residents of Lāna'i are Filipinos who work on "The World's Largest Pineapple Plantation." More than one million pineapples per day leave the harbor of Kaumalapau during the height of the summer harvest.

Lāna'i is a rough-hewn island, where the less-than-hardy tourist is not likely to be at ease. According to the state-approved "Lāna'i Plan," both development and tourism will be limited, and nearly 80 percent of the land will remain agricultural or open forest and meadowland.

Kaho'olawe, the smallest of Hawaii's eight major islands, is an uninhabited mass of red dirt seven miles southwest of Maui. Its history has been far from rosy. Once inhabited by fishermen, it has always been too dry to support much agriculture. In the early nineteenth century, the island was used as a penal colony. Later, it was given to raising sheep. In 1953, the United States Navy took it over for use as a target range. Bombing ended in 1980, when several sites on the island were listed on the National Register of Historic Places.

Most mysterious of all is the island at the eastern end of the Hawaiian Archipelago—tiny, "forbidden" Ni'ihau. Purchased from Kamehameha V in 1864 by the wealthy and reclusive Robinson family, it has, until recently, been "off limits" to visitors. Limited helicopter tours now allow a few visitors per year to meet the people and catch the flavor of this secret place.

Set in the lee of Kaua'i, Ni'ihau is arid and rocky and given mostly to raising cattle and sheep. At its center is 182-acre Lake Halāli'i, the largest natural lake in the Islands. Most of Ni'ihau's two hundred or so residents are Hawaiians who still speak their ancient tongue. There is one village, Pu'uwai, with one grammar school. To continue their education, students generally go from there to O'ahu or Kaua'i, usually to the Kamehameha Schools for Hawaiians.

Ni'ihau's residents live quietly, their island seemingly frozen in another time. The island has no public electrical power supply, no automobiles or paved roads, no liquor, and no jail. It is the only Island that voted solidly against statehood.

Some Ni'ihau residents gather honey or make charcoal from the island's kiawe wood. But one Ni'ihau product is absolutely unique. The women of Ni'ihau gather the tiny shells—burgundy, white, spotted, and brown—that wash ashore on their peaceful beaches and string them into intricate shell leis. Prized and worn proudly, these leis are considered works of art and sell for as much as two thousand dollars each.

Many smaller dots of land cluster around the eight major islands. However, the only ones likely to show up on a world map are Lehua, off the north coast of Ni'ihau, and Molokini, between Maui and Kaho'olawe. The island of Molokini is a favorite snorkeling destination, because its crescent-shaped crater shelters an amazing array of aquatic life.

The smallest of the Islands are destinations only for birds—bumps in the water with colorful, descriptive nicknames like Rabbit Island, Goat Island, and Chinaman's Hat, saluting their inhabitants or their shapes.

Beautiful sandy beach at the Kaluako'i Resort

Plumeria, found in many colors, grows throughout the Islands.

Remains of fishpond used by the ancient Hawaiians to raise and fatten saltwater fish

Lehua Islet with Niʻihau in the background, located nineteen miles off the southwest coast of Kauaʻi

Moaʻula Falls in Hālawa Valley on the eastern end of Molokaʻi

Windswept Kū-āhua Beach on the north shore of Lānaʻi

Old shipwreck off Shipwreck Beach on the island of Lāna'i

North coast of Moloka‘i

North coast of Moloka'i

Hālawa Congregational Church in quiet Hālawa Valley

Pūko'o Beach on the southwest coast of Moloka'i

Ancient Aliʻi Fishponds on the south coast of Molokaʻi

Old Church on the Kalaupapa Peninsula